INSIDE MAGIC

ABRACADABRA!
COOL MAGIC
TRICKS WITH
CARDS

Nicholas Einhorn

rosen publishing's
rosen
central

New York

This edition published in 2013 by:

The Rosen Publishing Group, Inc.
29 East 21st Street
New York, NY 10010

Library of Congress Cataloging-in-Publication Data

Einhorn, Nicholas.
Abracadabra!: cool magic tricks with cards/Nicholas Einhorn.
    p. cm.—(Inside magic)
Includes bibliographical references (p.   ) and index.
ISBN 978-1-4488-9219-8 (library binding)
1. Magic tricks—Juvenile literature. I. Title.
GV1548.E32 2013
793.8—dc23

2012028945

Manufactured in the United States of America

CPSIA Compliance Information: Batch #W13YA: For further information, contact Rosen Publishing, New York, New York, at 1-800-237-9932.

Copyright in design, text and images © Anness Publishing Limited, U.K. 2002, 2013. Originally published as part of a larger volume: *The Art of Magic.*

CONTENTS

Why are card tricks so popular? One reason could be that playing cards are internationally recognized symbols. Over the centuries people from the East shared their ideas and card tricks with people in the West, resulting in a universal familiarity with cards. Perhaps this explains why there are more card tricks published than any other type of magic.

Playing cards have a rich history. The first playing cards are thought to have been invented in the twelfth century in China. Their popularity spread quickly throughout the East. Playing cards probably began to appear in Europe at the end of the fourteenth century. They changed drastically as the original Eastern designs were replaced by European designs, which evolved as they passed from country to country.

It seems it was some time before it occurred to anyone that playing cards could be used for magic. A Spanish magician by the name of Dalmau performed card tricks for Emperor Charles V in Milan at the turn of the sixteenth century, and there is evidence to suggest that by the seventeenth century card magic was a popular form of entertainment. Queen Elizabeth I apparently enjoyed watching card tricks, and in 1602 she paid an Italian magician 200 crowns to perform for her.

The scope for creating illusions with a deck of cards is huge. As well as the "you pick a card, I'll find it" type of effect, many different illusions can be created using cards. As you will learn, they can be made to appear, disappear, change, multiply, defy gravity, and a lot more. Playing cards can generally be found in most homes and in many public places. It always pays to know a few card tricks so that when the opportunity arises, you can be ready to spring into action!

basic card techniques

For many of the techniques you will learn in the following pages, it is important for you to hold the deck in the correct way so that you can accomplish the moves with ease and success. The grips shown below are simple to master and should feel very natural after just a little practice. Do not let the names of the various grips worry you. They sound more complicated than they really are!

the hand

In order to fully understand how to handle a deck of cards, it is vital that you know which part of the hand is which.

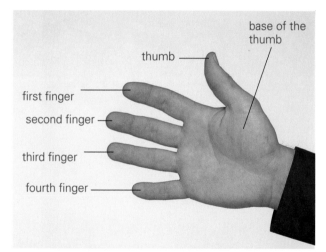

Although mostly self-explanatory, you may find that some of the magic terms used to describe the parts of the hand are unfamiliar to you. Therefore, before you continue, take a moment to check that you know which part of the hand is which.

dealing grip

In most instances you will be holding the deck as shown below. It is likely that you would hold a deck of cards like this instinctively.

The deck is clipped by the thumb in the left hand. All the fingers are located along the other long edge, known as the "side" of the deck. Notice how the thumb is positioned on the top of the deck and how the cards bevel slightly. In this position, it is possible for the thumb to push off cards individually from the top of the deck.

mechanics' grip

This variation of the Dealing Grip will allow certain moves to become possible. However, in most cases these two grips are interchangeable.

biddle grip

This is another simple grip that you will need to become familiar with in order to perform many of the sleights in this book.

The difference between this and the Dealing Grip is that the cards are held more firmly, with the left first finger curled around the top short edge of the deck (known as the end of the deck) and the thumb positioned straight along the left side of the deck.

Hold the deck from above in the right hand. The thumb holds the deck at the end nearest you. The first finger is curled gently on top of the deck, and the second and third fingers hold the deck at the end farthest from you.

dribbling cards

This is a simple flourish with a deck of cards. Learning to dribble will help you to become familiar with handling a deck comfortably. Aside from a simple flourish, the dribble can also be used to help make controlling a card more deceptive (see Injog Dribble Control, p. 41).

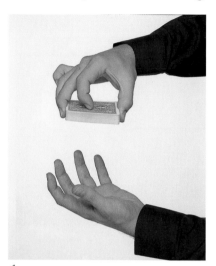

1. Hold the deck in the right-hand Biddle Grip position with the left hand in an open position below.

2. With the right first finger (curled on top of the deck), apply pressure as the right fingers and thumb simultaneously release pressure, allowing the cards to fall rapidly, one after the other, into the waiting left hand. Try experimenting with varying distances between your hands.

3. Cradle the cards in the left hand and square them to complete the flourish.

two-handed spread

This is simply a neat way to offer cards for a selection. It is a very basic technique, but one with which you should become familiar from the start. A nice spread of cards can be an early indication to your spectators that you are a polished performer.

1. Hold the cards using the left-hand Dealing Grip or Mechanics' Grip. The left thumb pushes the top few cards to the right.

2. The right hand approaches, gripping the spread of cards in the space between the thumb and base of the fingers, called the "crotch" in magic. The left fingers and thumb begin to push several more cards over to the right, the right fingers providing support from beneath.

3. Continue to push the cards with the left thumb as your hands stretch into an arc. The result is a neat and uniform spread of cards.

4. From underneath the spread, you can see how the cards are supported by the outstretched fingers of both hands.

squaring the cards

This is a simple procedure to ensure that the cards are neat, tidy and perfectly square. Very often, working with a deck of cards that has been neatly squared will make the learning process easier and facilitate general card handling.

1. Hold the untidy deck in the left hand. Start to square the cards so that you hold the deck in a loose Mechanics' Grip.

2. Approach the deck from above in the right-hand Biddle Grip position. Squeeze the ends of the deck together. Slide the right hand back and forth along the ends, and then support the deck in the Biddle Grip position while your left hand moves up and down.

3. The result is a deck of cards squared neatly in the left hand.

swing cut

This is a very useful cut that is simple to learn and is referred to in many of the routines in this book. The top card of the deck has been marked with a black border so that you can follow the sequence of the cut more clearly.

1. Hold the deck in the right-hand Biddle Grip position.

2. Extend the first finger so that it rests near the corner of the deck farthest from you.

3. With your first finger, lift half of the cards and pivot them out to the left. (Your right thumb is the pivot point.)

4. With your left hand, pinch the top half of the deck in the crotch of the thumb.

5. The result is a deck of cards squared neatly in the left hand.

charlier cut

This is a pretty, one-handed cut. It is relatively easy to master with just a little practice. If you experience difficulty with it, try altering your grip in the first step. Through trial and error, the Charlier Cut will become second nature to you.

1. Hold the deck up high on the left fingertips. Notice how the deck is held on all edges.

2. Releasing pressure from your thumb, allow approximately half of the deck to fall down toward the palm of your hand.

3. Your first finger should now curl under the deck and push the bottom packet of cards toward the thumb.

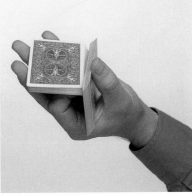

4. Let the bottom packet clear the top packet, which drops onto the curled first finger.

5. Close your thumb and fingers together to complete the cut. You can now use your right hand to help square the cards.

the glimpse

It is often necessary to secretly look at and remember a particular card in the deck. This secret move is known as a "glimpse." There are many ways to do this, depending on how the cards are being held. Two "glimpses" are explained here, enabling you to learn the bottom card of the deck secretly, in an unsuspicious way. You may be able to think of other subtle ways, too.

out of the box glimpse

An ideal time to "glimpse" a card occurs when you are removing the cards from the card box. Simply ensure that the deck is oriented so that it is pulled out of the box faceup. Absolutely no attention should be drawn to the deck at this stage. If required, a casual Overhand Shuffle gives you an extra opportunity to move the "glimpsed" card to another location, such as the top of the deck.

square and glimpse

This is another way to secretly look at the bottom card of the deck while handling the cards in a natural way. The "glimpse" takes place during the innocent action of squaring the deck. All the movements occur in one smooth action. Essentially you are squaring the deck while turning it from end to end. It is so subtle, your audience will never suspect a thing!

1. Hold the deck facedown in the left hand, with the right hand supporting the deck in the Biddle Grip. The deck is squared.

2. With the right hand, lift the deck and turn it palm up by twisting at the wrist. Simultaneously turn the left hand palm down so that it can continue the squaring action along the sides of the deck. The bottom card of the deck will now be facing you, and this is when you "glimpse" the card.

3. Almost immediately, lift the deck with the left hand and turn it palm up again as the right hand turns palm down, back to the start position. The hands square the cards one final time.

the braue reversal

A magician named Frederick Braue created this simple way to reverse a card in the center of the deck. Here, the top card of the deck is reversed. Performed quickly, the Braue Reversal simply looks like a series of quick cuts and should not arouse any suspicion.

Secret View

1. Hold the deck in right-hand Biddle Grip with a Thumb Break under the top card. For ease of explanation, there is a black border on the top card.

Secret View

2. With the left hand, take the bottom half of the deck and turn it faceup, flipping it on top of the right-hand cards.

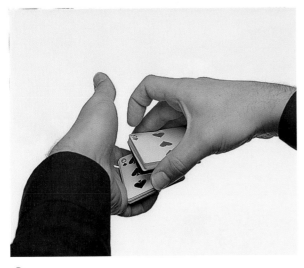

3. Allow all the remaining cards below the break to fall into the left hand. These are again reversed and replaced under the right-hand cards.

4. Spread the deck between your hands. The result will be that the top card of the deck has been reversed in the center.

tip This method of reversing a card can also be used to reveal a selected card. Have a card returned to the deck and controlled to the top. Now perform the Braue Reversal and spread the deck onto the table to display one card reversed. It will be the one selected.

the glide

This is a useful move, creating the illusion that the bottom card of the deck has been removed when in reality the second card from the bottom is removed. This simple procedure is worth learning if only for Gliding Home (p. 46), which is a wonderful trick.

1. Hold the deck in the left hand from above. The deck should be held by the sides, thumb on the right side and fingers on the left. Hold the cards high enough to allow the first joints of the fingers to bend around the deck and rest on the bottom card.

Secret View

2. This view from underneath shows how the extreme tips of the fingers are positioned on the face of the card.

Secret View

3. Drag the bottom card back about 1/4–1/2 in (5–10 mm) by pulling the second, third and fourth fingers backward. (The first finger remains stationary.) The bottom card remains aligned against the left thumb.

Secret View

4. The right hand approaches palm up and reaches under the deck to supposedly remove the bottom card. What actually happens is that the second card is removed instead. The tips of the right fingers drag the second card forward, facilitated by the overlap created by the Glide.

tip The Glide is not seen from the front. It is a secret move that remains hidden under the deck. An alternative method is to approach the deck with the right hand and push the bottom card back a fraction of a second before the second card is pulled forward.

double lift and turnover

The Double Lift and Turnover is another essential sleight to master if you wish to become a competent cardician. Theoretically the procedure is simple, but putting the theory into effect will take plenty of practice. In theory a "double lift" is the name given to the concept of lifting two cards and displaying them as one. The technique is used to achieve many results, a few of which are explored in the explanations that follow.

There are enough techniques and variations to the turning of two cards as one to fill this entire book. The truth is, every individual finds a technique that is comfortable for him or her and sticks with it. Further reading will enable you to explore different options, and with time you will find small changes that suit you. As long as your Double Lift is convincing, it does not really matter which technique you choose.

There a few important points to be aware of. The setup should remain unseen. The turning of the two cards should look natural and arouse no suspicion. In other words, don't say "Here is the top card of the deck," because as soon as you say that, people will start to wonder if it really is the top card of the deck. If you just show it, perhaps saying the card's name out loud, people will just assume it is the top card. You must create a reason for placing the card back onto the deck after the first display.

Secret View

2. While the first finger is curled around the end of the deck farthest from you, the second and third fingers stretch out and begin to pull the cards flush again, but as this happens, the fourth finger separates the top two cards of the deck.

Secret View

1. The Double Lift requires a setup. It is necessary to separate the top two cards from the rest of the deck. In order to achieve this, hold the deck in left-hand Mechanics' Grip. The left thumb pushes off the top few cards, to the right, in a spread.

3. The deck should now be held, squared, in the left hand with a Finger Break (p. 39), as shown, under the top two cards.

Secret View

4. The view from the front reveals nothing. The cards are simply held in the Mechanics' Grip with a Finger Break below the top two cards.

5. The right hand approaches the deck in Biddle Grip position. The gap created by the Finger Break enables only the top two cards to be lifted. The right first finger pushes gently on the back of the card(s) to keep them aligned.

6. The right hand turns at the wrist to reveal the face of the card. It is mistaken for the top card of the deck, but in reality it is the second card from the top.

7. After the display, turn the wrist again, and replace the card(s) back onto the top of the deck. Snap your fingers or make a magical gesture, and pick up the real top card of the deck, turning it over to reveal that the card has mysteriously changed.

snap change

This is a visually stunning sleight, which takes only a little practice to perfect. With a snap of the fingers, one card instantly changes into another. It is recommended that you learn this sleight so that if a card trick ever goes wrong, you can simply ask which card was chosen and spread through the deck, cutting the selector's card second from the top. Show the top card as an "indifferent" card, perform the Snap Change, and magically change the indifferent card into the one selected. Magicians call these types of scenarios "outs"; that is, they can get the magician out of trouble if a trick goes wrong.

Secret View

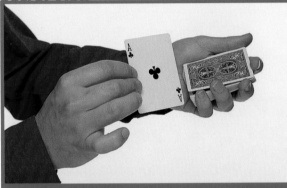

1. Show the top card of the deck (in this example the Ace of Clubs). Secretly obtain a Finger Break under the top card in the left hand.

Secret View

2. Lay the Ace of Clubs faceup and square on to the deck.

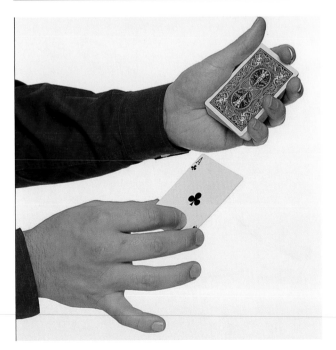

3. The Finger Break will enable you to pick up the top two cards with ease. The two cards are held together as one between the right thumb and second finger at the extreme end. The first finger is bent on top.

4. Move the card(s) under your elbow and temporarily out of sight.

5. Squeeze the two cards, allowing them to flick off the second finger so that the cards flip over and are pinched at the lower right corner by the thumb and first finger. The cards should still be perfectly aligned.

6. Immediately bring the cards into sight and place them back on to the top of the deck where they can be squared. The card will be seen to have changed.

7. Turn the top card facedown to complete the sleight. This is a speedy and highly visual piece of magic.

ribbon spread and turnover

This is a lovely flourish, pretty to watch and a sign of a magician who can handle a deck of cards. The cards are spread and displayed in a neat facedown line, and then caused to flip faceup "domino-style." You will find it easier to perform with a deck of cards in good condition and on a soft surface such as a tablecloth or close-up mat. You will also need a clear space to ensure a smooth spread.

1. Hold the deck face-down in the right-hand Biddle Grip. Place the deck flat on the table at your far left.

2. Stretch out your first finger so that it rests on the side of the deck and just brushes the surface of the table. Pull the deck to the right a bit, and the deck will naturally bevel.

3. Begin moving your hand to the right at an even pace with even pressure. With the first finger, regulate the distance between each card as you continue to spread the deck in a straight line until all the cards are spread out.

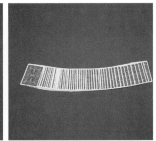

4. The result is an even spread of cards in a relatively straight line. With practice, you will be able to spread the cards instantly, in under a second, and with absolute precision.

5. To turn the cards faceup, lift the edge of the cards at the far left of the spread and run your first finger along the edges so that the spread begins to turn faceup "domino-style."

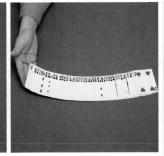

6. When you reach the end of the spread, allow the last cards to drop faceup onto your palm in preparation for the final step. Do not let the cards fall flat onto the table.

7. Now move the right hand to the left, scooping up the deck into one pile. Lift this pile off the table.

8. Finish the sequence by squaring the cards with both hands, and continue with your next card trick or flourish.

shuffling cards

Very often you can impress your audience before you even begin a single trick by handling the cards in a way that suggests you have spent considerable time and effort practicing. Apart from the Weave Shuffle and Waterfall, these shuffles are not too difficult to master. Indeed, you may be familiar with them already. Often several shuffles are required to thoroughly mix the deck.

overhand shuffle

This is arguably the most commonly used and easiest shuffle. These moves are repeated over and over with varying numbers of cards until you are satisfied the deck has been shuffled. Due to the fact that the cards are being mixed in small packets, it will take a lot of shuffling to ensure a very thorough disruption of the sequence of cards.

1. Hold the deck with one of its sides along the creases at the base of the left fingers. The thumb naturally rests on the back of the deck, and the fingers do likewise on the front.

2. With the right hand, approach from above and pick up approximately the bottom three-quarters of the deck.

3. In a chopping motion, bring the right hand back to the deck and deposit half the cards on top of the deck. Then bring the right hand away with the other half.

4. Finally, with one more chop, deposit the remainder of the cards on the top.

table riffle shuffle

This is an effective and professional way to shuffle a deck of cards. By controlling the cards as they fall, you can ensure that the last group of cards are "riffled" off the right thumb. Any cards within this group (which was on the top of the deck at the beginning) will be on top of the deck at the end of the shuffle. The Riffle Shuffle can thus be used as a false shuffle, allowing you to keep cards at the top of the deck.

1. The deck should be squared and lying on the table, side toward you. With the right hand, cut off approximately half of the cards.

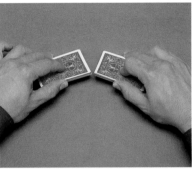

2. Place this packet to the right of the bottom half and mirror your grip with the left hand. With the thumbs of both hands, lift up the back edges. Notice how the corners almost touch. The front edges of the deck rest on the table.

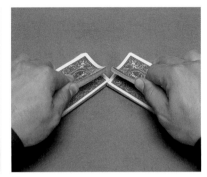

3. Slowly allow the cards to riffle off both thumbs. As this happens, nudge both packets together.

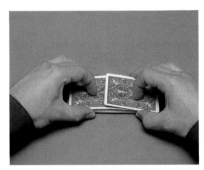

5. Change your grip so that you can push both packets together completely by applying pressure along the ends of the deck with both first fingers while simultaneously squaring the cards with your thumbs on the side nearest you.

4. When this riffle is complete, push each packet into the other about halfway.

6. The result is a shuffled, squared deck that is then ready for your next miracle.

weave shuffle and waterfall

This shuffle looks fantastic when it is performed smoothly. It creates the impression that you are a master cardsharp! You must use a deck of cards in perfect condition because you are relying on the corners of the deck to ensure a good weave. If the edges of the individual cards are split or damaged, you will find this shuffle very difficult. With enough practice, you will be able to split the cards into exactly two packets of 26 and shuffle them so accurately that every card will be woven in the opposite direction to its neighbor. Professional magicians know this as the Perfect Faro Shuffle. If you can achieve this degree of accuracy every time, you will be able to master almost any sleight-of-hand card trick you may come across in the future. The end result is well worth the effort you need to put in.

1. Make sure the cards are perfectly square. Hold them high up on the tips of the left fingers, as shown here.

2. With the right hand, approach the deck from above. The first finger is held straight out and rests on the end of the deck farthest from you.

3. With the right thumb, second and third fingers cut and lift half of the deck up and away from the lower packet.

4. Tap this top half gently against the end of the bottom half, to ensure that the edges of both packets are perfectly square.

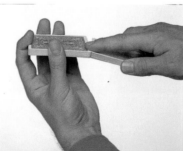

5. Place the corners nearest you against each other. Notice at this stage how only the corners in the front touch, and how the first finger of the right hand keeps the packets perfectly level with each other.

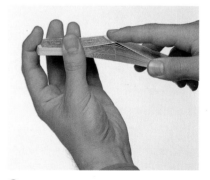

6. Gently push the corners together, and the cards will begin to weave, as shown here. (You may find that a slight back-and-forth motion will ease the cards into the weave.)

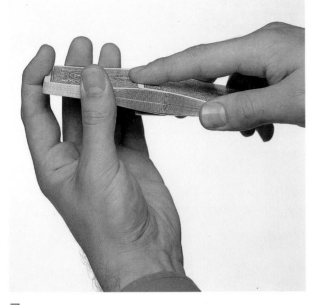

7. Push the packets together so that approximately one-quarter of the cards overlap.

8. Adjust the left hand's grip by moving your thumb, third, and fourth fingers down to the woven section. This gives you the ability to hold the deck in one hand.

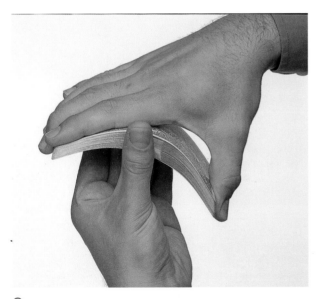

9. Stretch the right hand wide open and approach the deck from above. Your thumb should grip the end nearest you, with the fingers on the end farthest away.

10. Release the left hand's grip, and squeeze the cards into an arc with the right hand. The cards will cascade inward, producing a lovely waterfall pattern as they fall. Keep the left hand underneath, just in case the cards start to slip. Finish by squaring the deck neatly.

self-working card tricks

It is important to realize that although self-working card tricks are relatively easy to perform, they do require a certain amount of human input and will not work unless the various steps are followed correctly. The advantage of self-working tricks is that you can spend less time learning the mechanics of the trick and more time working on an entertaining presentation.

sense of touch

After performing a few card tricks, state that it is possible to develop super-sensitivity in your fingertips. As a demonstration, shuffle the cards and hold them facedown. The top card is held with its back toward the magician, yet by feeling its face it is possible to identify the card every time. Explain that your sensitive fingers allow you to know whether the card is black or red, and how many pips (symbols) are on it.

1. From a shuffled deck, deal one card facedown into your right hand and hold it in front of you at about neck level. Hold it by the thumb at the bottom edge and the fingers at the top edge, with its back toward you. Your left first finger moves up to touch the face of the card.

2. This shows the view from behind. As the finger touches the face of the card for the first time, gently squeeze your right fingers and thumb. This will begin to bend or bow the card backward.

Secret View

3. The left finger is omitted here so that you can clearly see what happens. The card is bowed just enough for you to glimpse the lower left index.

the four burglars

This classic trick is accompanied by a story. Four jacks are shown to be at the top of the deck, and one by one they are placed separately into different positions. The four jacks magically return to the top.

Read through the steps with your cards in hand until you are familiar with the order of the steps. Then learn the patter and match up the words to the moves. When learned and performed confidently, this will become a charming addition to your repertoire, and it is sure to get a great reaction every time it is performed.

1. Secretly remove any three cards plus the four jacks.

2. Hold the jacks in a fan, with the extra three cards squared neatly below the lowest one.

3. Begin by displaying the four jacks to the audience. (They should be unaware of the extra cards.)

4. Neatly square the cards in the left hand, being careful to hide the extra thickness along the edge of the cards.

5. Turn the packet of cards face-down and place them on top of the deck.

6. Take the top card of the deck and, without showing its face, push it into the deck approximately ten cards from the bottom. Leave it protruding half its length.

7. Take the new top card and push it into the deck at the half-way point. Leave it protruding as before.

8. Repeat with the new top card, inserting it about ten cards from the top of the deck.

9. Turn the top card faceup to show a jack, and then replace it facedown but protruding from the top of the deck.

10. Slowly push all four cards neatly and squarely into the deck.

11. Dribble the cards from hand to hand, matching your actions to your patter.

12. Deal the top four cards faceup to show that the jacks have returned.

the story: (The numbers correspond to the above steps.)
"There were four burglars named Jack who decided to try to burgle a house (3, 4, 5). The first burglar broke into the basement (6), the second managed to enter the kitchen (7), and the third burglar climbed through an open window in a bedroom (8). The last burglar stayed on the roof to look out for the police (9). As each of the burglars entered the house (10), the lookout on the roof saw a police car driving toward them. He called his three friends (11), who immediately ran up to the roof, slid down the drainpipe, and made their escape (12)."

hocus pocus

Twenty-one cards are dealt onto the table, and one is thought of by the spectator. After a short process of dealing the cards, the magic words "hocus pocus" are used to find the selection. This is one of the best-known card tricks, but it still amazes everyone who sees it. Although the principle and method are mathematical, it requires no skill or mathematics on the part of the magician. Better yet, it works every single time as long as the steps are followed in the correct order. Try this out with the cards in hand, and you may even amaze yourself!

1. Deal three cards faceup from left to right (as if you were dealing a round of cards to three people).

2. Deal another three cards in exactly the same way. Continue until you have three columns of seven cards – 21 cards in all. Ask the spectator to remember any one of the cards. In our example, the chosen card is the Queen of Diamonds.

3. Ask the spectator to tell you which column the chosen card is in. (In our example, it is in column number three.) Pick up one of the other piles, and then pick up the chosen pile and place it on top.

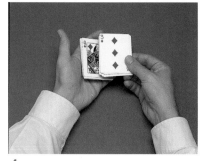

4. Finally pick up the last pile, adding it to the others. Remember the golden rule: the chosen column must be placed in the middle of the other two.

5. Deal three cards from the top of the packet as you did at the beginning, but holding the packet faceup.

6. Continue dealing until all the cards have once again been dealt.

7. Ask the spectator to confirm which column his card is in this time. As before, pick up all three columns, ensuring that the chosen column goes between the other two

8. Re-deal the cards in exactly the same fashion as before. Ask the spectator one final time which column contains his card. Collect the cards as before.

9. Turn the cards facedown and explain that to find the selected card, you need to use the ancient magic words "hocus pocus." Deal the cards onto the table, spelling out loud, one letter for each card.

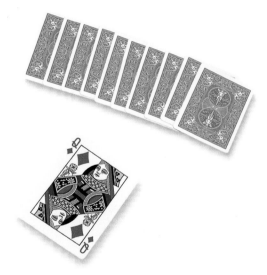

10. The very next card will be the one selected. Ask for the name of the chosen card, and turn the top card over.

11. Show that the selection has been found and that the magic word has worked.

tip After the process of dealing has been repeated three times, the mentally selected card will automatically be the eleventh card down from the top of the facedown packet. This means you could use any word with ten or eleven letters to find the selection, so with a little thought you can personalize this trick. You may be able to use your name, your spectator's name, or the name of a school or organization.

reversed

A card is chosen and inserted back into the deck. You explain that you will demonstrate the fastest trick in the world. You then place the cards behind your back for a split second. When they are brought to the front again, you spread the cards and one is seen reversed in the center. It is the card selected.

This is a typical example of a very simple method used to accomplish what seems like a miracle. Performed well, this effect cannot fail to win over an audience.

1. The setup is simple and will take one second to accomplish. Secretly reverse the bottom card faceup under the facedown deck.

2. Spread the facedown deck between your hands, and ask for a card to be selected. Take care that the bottom card is not seen to be reversed.

3. While the card selected is being looked at and remembered by the spectator, secretly turn the deck upside down. To make this easier, you could explain that you will turn your back so that you cannot see the selected card. When your back is turned, reverse the deck.

4. Because of the card reversed earlier, the deck will still appear to be facedown. Make sure the deck is perfectly squared, and then ask the spectator to push her card somewhere into the middle of the deck.

Secret View

5. Announce that you will demonstrate the world's fastest trick. Move the cards behind your back. As soon as they are out of sight, push the top card off the deck and turn the whole deck over on top of this card.

6. Bring the deck to the front again, and it will look as if nothing has changed. The deck will still appear facedown. Spread the cards between your hands or ribbon-spread them across a table to show that there is one card reversed.

7. The reversed card will be the one selected. Turn it facedown again, and continue with another trick.

the indicator

A card is chosen and returned to the deck. The deck is spread, and one card is found reversed. Although it is not the card selected, it acts as an indicator and helps to find it.

This is a good example of how a key card is used to achieve a certain goal, that is, finding the selection. Once you understand the principle involved, you can use any card as the "indicator" and simply adjust the setup accordingly. For example, if the Five of Hearts is used, the reversed card needs to be set five cards from the bottom.

1. The setup is easy to remember. Reverse any eight and position it eight cards from the bottom of the deck. This is a secret setup, so the reversed card should remain hidden.

2. Fan the cards for a selection, but do not spread them too far in case the reversed card is prematurely exposed. With a small amount of practice, the cards can be handled relatively freely.

3. While the card is being looked at, swing-cut the top half of the deck into the left hand.

4. Have the selected card replaced on top of the left-hand cards, and then place the right-hand cards on top of it.

Secret View

5. Riffle the end of the deck, explaining that one card will reverse itself.

6. Spread the deck and show the eight reversed in the center. Cut the deck at this point, bringing the eight to the top of the deck. The selector will be quick to tell you it is the wrong card.

7. Explain that the eight is merely an indicator card and indicates to you that the chosen card is in fact eight cards down from the top.

8. Place the eight to one side, and count off seven cards one at a time, out loud. Turn over the eighth card. It will be the card selected.

instant card revelation

A card is chosen and returned to the deck in the fairest manner. Without hesitation, the magician is able to reveal the chosen card. This effect takes advantage of a "glimpsed" card. It should be performed briskly and, as you will see, you do not even need to pull the chosen card out of the deck; you can simply say the name of the card out loud. For some reason, it seems more impossible if you just say the name of the card, as opposed to physically finding it. Try both ways and see which method you prefer.

1. Using one of the techniques explained, "glimpse" and remember the bottom card of the deck (in this example, the King of Hearts). This becomes your key card.

2. Spread the cards for a selection, emphasizing the fairness of the choice open to the spectator.

3. Ask for the selected card to be remembered (in this example, the Five of Diamonds). Simultaneously square the deck.

4. Swing-cut the top half of the deck into your left hand.

5. Have the card replaced onto your left-hand cards, and then place the right hand's cards on top, positioning your key card above the selection.

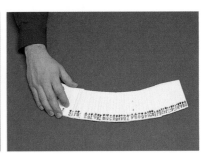

6. You can make a quick faceup Ribbon Spread along the surface of the table, or spread the cards between your hands, toward you.

7. Either way, find your key card, and the selected card will be the one directly above it. Remove it from the spread and reveal the selection.

the next card is yours

A card is chosen and returned to the deck. The magician deals the cards one at a time, faceup onto the table. While dealing, he states that the next card to be turned over will be the one selected. Even though the spectators are sure the magician has failed, since they have seen that the selected card has already been dealt, much to their amusement and surprise, the next card to be turned over is in fact the selected card. This trick is a "sucker" trick – your audience thinks the trick has gone wrong, but it is really part of the presentation.

1. Secretly "glimpse" the bottom card of the deck, using one of the methods described earlier. This will be your key card. (In our example, it is the Ten of Diamonds.)

2. Using the Two-Handed Spread, offer the cards to a spectator for a selection.

3. Cut half of the deck to the table, and have the selected card placed on top of this packet. As you place the other half on top to bury the spectator's card, you will automatically position your key card directly above his selection. Cut the deck and complete the cut a few times, but do not shuffle!

4. Deal the cards faceup, one at a time. When you see your key card, the very next card dealt will be the one selected, but do not pause; continue dealing about ten more cards. Then say, "I bet you the next card I turn over will be yours." The spectator will immediately accept the bet.

5. Wait a second or two, and then watch the spectator's face as you reach for the card immediately next to your key card, which will of course be the one selected.

6. Turn it over, and you will win the bet! You will definitely have fun with this one!

do as I do

Two decks of cards are used. Both the magician and the spectator choose a card from their respective decks, and then put them back into the center. The decks are swapped and each looks for their selection. Both cards are placed side by side, and despite the odds against it happening, the cards mysteriously match each other. This is one of the cleverest cards tricks ever invented. Try it and you will amaze everyone who watches it. It simply defies explanation, and has become one of the all-time classic card tricks.

1. Give a deck of cards to the spectator, and keep a second deck for yourself. Have both shuffled. As you shuffle your deck, remember the bottom card. This is your key card.

2. Swap decks so that you now know the card on the bottom of the pile in front of the spectator. Explain that he must copy every move you make as closely as possible.

4. Pick up the card you cut to, and instruct the spectator to remember his. Look at your card, although you do not need to remember it. Just pretend to do so.

3. Cut approximately half the deck to your right. The spectator will mirror your actions.

5. Place the card back on the right-hand pile. Your spectator will copy you.

6. Place the left packet on top of the right. The spectator's card is now directly under your key card. At this point you can cut the cards as many times as you wish, although it is not necessary to do so.

7. Swap the decks again, and comment to your spectator on the absolute fairness with which you have both chosen a card.

8. Tell the spectator to find his chosen card at the same time that you find yours. Spread through the deck until you see your key card. The card immediately above it will be the one selected.

9. Place your card facedown on the table in front of you. The spectator will do likewise.

10. Explain that you both made the same moves at exactly the same time and so in theory you should have arrived at the same result. Turn over the cards to show a perfect match.

impossible card location

A deck of cards is split in two and thoroughly shuffled by two spectators. Each chooses and exchanges a card. The cards are shuffled again. Incredibly, and without hesitation, the magician is able to find both cards immediately.

The more your spectators try to figure out how you achieved this, the more impossible it will seem. The secret preparation is actually shown as part of the presentation of the trick, but it is so subtle that it remains absolutely invisible!

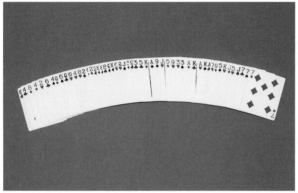

1. Set the deck by dividing all the odd cards from all the even cards. Place one set on top of the other. Spread or fan the deck toward two spectators, and explain that although the cards are already mixed, you want to have them mixed some more. A casual glance at the set-up cards will not be enough to see that the deck has been split into odd and even cards.

2. Split the deck at the point where the odd cards meet the even cards. Hand half the deck to each spectator. Ask them to shuffle their cards well. Really stress to the spectators that they can mix the cards as much as they like. This apparent fairness simply enhances the overall effect.

3. Request that the cards are spread out on the table facedown and that one from each half be chosen, remembered, and swapped with the other person's selection.

4. The selected cards are then placed back somewhere in the middle of the half opposite from where they came.

5. Have both half decks shuffled well again, and reiterate the fairness of the procedure thus far. Ask the spectators to leave the half decks squared on the table in front of them.

6. Pick up one packet and spread through it with the faces of the cards toward you. It will be easy to find the chosen card as it will be the only even card in the odd packet. Remove it and place it in front of the spectator who chose that card.

7. Repeat the same procedure with the second packet, placing the second selection in front of the other spectator. A little acting ability will go a long way at this point. Make it look as though you are having trouble finding the chosen card, or perhaps you can just start eliminating individual cards, scattering them to the table one at a time until there is only one card remaining in your hand.

8. Ask the spectators to verify the names of their cards. Turn each card over, and show that you correctly divined the selections. The ease of the method used for this trick allows you to focus on the presentation. Experiment with different styles until you find one that suits you.

magic time

A prediction is made and placed in the center of the table. A random hour in the day is thought of by a spectator. Twelve cards are laid in the formation of a clockface, and a card is chosen to represent the thought-of hour. The magician reveals the thought-of hour, and the prediction in the center of the table is found to match the chosen card.

This trick works on a mathematical principle and is very clever. Try it with a deck of cards in hand and you will amaze yourself! At the end of the explanation, there is a variation of the first method, using a marked card. This has the advantage of being even more deceptive.

1. The only preparation is to remember which card is thirteenth from the top of the deck. In our example, it is the Three of Diamonds.

2. Set the deck facedown on the table, and write a prediction on a piece of paper, with a question mark on the back. Your prediction is the card you remembered. Place it on the table, with the question mark facing up, not letting the audience see your prediction.

3. Ask someone to think of their favorite hour of the day, and to take that many cards off the top of the deck and put them on the bottom. Turn your back while this happens so that there is no way for you to know what hour it is. Let us assume that person thinks of 4 o'clock, and move four cards from the top to the bottom.

4. Take the deck and deal twelve cards onto the table, reversing their order.

6. Your prediction card will automatically position itself at the thought-of hour. However, do not reveal it just yet. Build up the suspense by asking the spectator which wrist he wears his watch on. Ask him to hold that wrist over the center of the circle. Hold his wrist as if trying to pick up a psychic vibe, indicating what hour he chose. Reveal the thought-of hour.

5. Pick up this pile and set the cards out faceup in a clock formation around your prediction so that the first card you deal is at 1 o'clock, the second at 2 o'clock, etc. (The 12 o'clock position should be placed so that it is the farthest card from the spectator.)

7. Ask the spectator to confirm that you are correct, then call attention to the card at his chosen hour (in this case, 4 o'clock). It will be the Three of Diamonds.

8. Turn over your prediction to show a perfect match.

9. If you mark the back of the thirteenth card (Three of Diamonds), you can lay the cards facedown instead of faceup. As the cards are dealt, the marked card will indicate the thought-of hour.

10. This close-up view of the card shows the normal design compared to the subtle mark, which is easy to spot if you are aware of it. Part of the design on the back of the card has been filled in with a permanent marker pen that matches the color of the card.

11. At step 7, after the thought-of hour is revealed and confirmed as being correct, reverse the appropriate card at the thought-of hour.

spectator cuts the aces

A deck of cards is placed in front of the spectator, who cuts it into approximately four equal packets. Although the magician never touches the deck and the spectator mixes the cards some more, the top card of each packet is found to be an ace.

Four-ace tricks are very popular with magicians. In fact, four-of-a-kind tricks make up a large percentage of card tricks. This self-working card trick is amazing; the method is simple and the impact on an audience is powerful.

1. To prepare, secretly find the four aces and move them to the top of the deck.

2. Place the deck on a table and invite a spectator to cut it into two approximately equal halves. Keep track of the original top of the deck at all times (that is, the packet with the four Aces at the top).

3. Ask the spectator to cut one of the packets in half again, and indicate where she is to place the cards.

4. Ask for the other half-deck to be cut in half again in the opposite direction, indicating both verbally and with your hand where the final packet should go. Make sure you still know which pile has the four aces on top.

5. You should have four approximately equal packets in front of you. The four aces should be on the top of one of the end packets, depending on which way the cards were cut. In our example, the four aces are on the top of the packet on the far right. Explain that four random points in the deck have been found.

6. Point to the packet at the end opposite to the aces. Ask the spectator to pick up the deck and to move three cards from the top to the bottom. The fact that the spectator makes all the moves increases the apparent fairness of the whole procedure.

7. Now tell your spectator to deal one card from the top of the packet in her hand to each of the piles on the table, in any order she wishes.

8. Having replaced the first packet, the spectator should pick up the second packet and repeat the same procedure; that is, take three cards from the top and place them at the bottom. She should deal one card to the top of each packet on the table.

9. This exact sequence should be repeated with the third packet. Each time explain which moves to make and watch to ensure that the spectator follows your instructions correctly. If any wrong moves are made, it may be because you did not explain the procedure clearly enough.

10. The fourth packet is treated in exactly the same way. This will result in four packets facedown on the table, which you have not touched from the very beginning.

11. Explain the randomness of the cuts and that without even touching the cards you have been able to influence the actions taken. Turn over one of the cards on the top of one of the packets. It will be an ace.

tip During the sequence of movements what actually happens is that you add three cards on top of the aces, move those three added cards to the bottom and deal one ace to each of the other three piles. All of the other moves are simply a smoke screen to help hide the method!

12. Turn over the top cards of the remaining three packets, revealing an ace on each.

spell-a-card

A card is selected and replaced in the deck. The magician seems to be in trouble and fails to find the chosen card. It is suggested that maybe the card will answer to its name in the same way that a dog would! The cards are dealt one at a time onto the table, one card for each letter. The final card proves to be the one selected. This is yet another example of how the use of a key card can create a different effect.

1. Secretly "glimpse" the bottom card of the deck. This will become your key card. In this case it is the Three of Hearts.

2. Using a Two-Handed Spread, offer the cards to a spectator for a selection.

3. Swing-cut the top half of the deck and have the selected card replaced onto the original top card. Place the rest of the deck on top, positioning the key card directly above the selection.

4. You can give the cards a false shuffle at this point, as long as the selected card and key card stay side by side. Spread through the deck faceup, and explain that you are going to find the selected card. Find your key card. The card above it will be the one selected. In this case, the chosen card is the Five of Hearts.

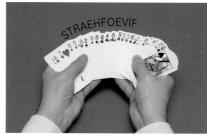

5. Starting from the selected card, begin to mentally spell its name. For every letter, move one card to the left. This is done as the cards are spread and should be practiced until you can do it without concentrating too much. When you reach the final letter, ask if you have passed the selected card. The spectator will tell you that you have and will think something has gone wrong. Cut the deck, and complete the cut at the card reached on the last letter. It is possible you may reach the top of the deck before you have finished spelling (see Tip for this eventuality).

6. Turn the deck facedown, and ask for the name of the selected card. When it is given to you, start dealing the cards facedown to the table one at a time, one card for each letter. The card that is dealt on the final letter will be the one selected.

tip Occasionally, you may run out of cards when spelling the name of the selected card. This is because you cut too deeply when the selected card was replaced. Just continue spelling from the face of the deck, acting as if you need to go through the deck again. Cut the cards as before and continue.

controlling a card

One of the most important sleights to learn is how to control a chosen card to the top of the deck. It will give you the ability to perform literally hundreds of different card tricks. Discussed here are several ways to control a card. It is always better to learn one really well than to learn several badly. In order to learn how to control a card, it is also important to understand a few other techniques and grips.

finger break

This break is used in a great number of tricks. It is one of the sleights most widely used by professional card magicians, predominantly for keeping control of a desired number of cards and also to aid the shift of the required cards from one position to another. It is an essential sleight that must be mastered if further study of card magic appeals to you. Because it uses the fourth finger, this particular sleight is also known as the Pinkie Break. It is not too difficult to learn, and it is worth learning well.

Secret View

1. Hold the deck in the left-hand Mechanics' Grip or Dealing Grip. With the right hand, approach from above in the Biddle Grip position and using the right thumb, lift approximately half of the cards about ½ in (1 cm). Release the cards, but allow the pad of the left fourth fingertip to stop the cards from falling flush.

2. The gap between the two packets need not be large – just enough for you to locate it at a future point in the particular routine. If pressure is applied from the thumb on top of the deck, the gap will close enough to remain hidden from both the front and sides.

Secret View

1. Hold a Finger Break as described above. With the right hand, approach the left hand from above and pick up the deck in the Biddle Grip position. However, as the thumb grips the back end (nearest you), the gap between the two packets is maintained by squeezing lightly between the right thumb and fingers. The cards are held entirely by the right hand, freeing the left hand.

thumb break

The Thumb Break is similar to the Finger Break and is used for the same purposes – to maintain control, or to aid the repositioning of certain cards. It is a vital sleight to learn, but you will be pleased to know that it is not at all difficult and will take no more than one or two trials to understand. It's even easier than the Finger Break!

double cut

The purpose of a Double Cut is to bring a card or block of cards from the middle of the deck to the top. It is a very useful move to master and, as you will learn, can also be used to control a selected card to the top of the deck.

1. Using the right hand, hold a Thumb Break about halfway down the deck. Drop approximately the bottom quarter of the deck into the left hand.

2. Grip these cards between the thumb and first finger and replace them on top of the right-hand cards.

3. Almost immediately loosen the right thumb's grip, letting the remaining cards (up to the Thumb Break) fall onto the fingers of the left hand.

4. Replace the left hand's packet onto the top of the right-hand cards in exactly the same way. The cards that were immediately below the Thumb Break are now on top of the deck. Square the deck and the Double Cut is complete.

double cut control

The Double Cut is also a neat and effective way to control a selected card to a desired position in the deck. The same set of moves are seen here to show how the card is controlled to the top. Performed swiftly, it allows you to control the selected card in an unsuspicious and smooth manner. Your audience will assume you are merely cutting the deck to mix the cards further. No attention should be called to the sequence of cuts. Study and practice this until it becomes second nature. The selected card is marked with a black border so that it can be easily followed throughout the explanation. This is one of the easiest, quickest ways to control a card to the top of the deck.

1. Assume you have had a card selected. Cut off half the deck (in the Biddle Grip) and have the selected card replaced onto the bottom half.

2. As the top half is replaced, hold a Thumb Break between the two packets. You will now perform the Double Cut as explained previously, that is, drop approximately the bottom quarter of the deck into the left hand. The left hand begins to move away with the dropped cards.

3. These cards are gripped between the thumb and first finger and are replaced on top of the right-hand cards. Almost immediately, the right thumb loosens its grip, letting the remaining cards (up to the Thumb Break) fall onto the fingers of the left hand. The top card of this dropped packet is the one selected.

4. Replace the left-hand packet onto the top of the right-hand cards in exactly the same way. The selected card is now on top of the deck.

injog dribble control

This addition to the Double Cut Control gives a very convincing touch of extra subtlety to the overall look of the sequence. The casualness with which the cards are handled will convince your audience that the selected card is lost in the deck.

1. Have a card selected. Cut off half the deck (in the Biddle Grip) and have the selected card replaced onto the bottom half. Dribble the cards from the right hand onto the selected card, ensuring that the first few cards are dribbled slightly toward you.

2. This view shows how the remaining cards are dribbled as the right hand moves forward so that the last group of cards fall square with the rest of the deck. The overlap of the cards seen in the above photo is known to magicians as an "injog."

3. As the right hand positions itself onto the top of the deck, allow the thumb to lift up the cards above the "injog" and secure a Thumb Break between the two packets. From here on, the Double Cut sequence is identical to that explained previously.

4. Drop approximately the bottom quarter of the deck into the left hand.

5. Grip these cards between the thumb and first finger, and replace them on top of the right-hand cards. Almost immediately, loosen the right thumb's grip, letting the remaining cards (up to the Thumb Break) fall onto the fingers of the left hand. The top card of this dropped packet is the one selected.

6. Replace the left-hand packet onto the top of the right-hand cards in exactly the same way. The result is that the selected card is now on top of the deck.

run and back control

This is yet another way to control a card, and it looks like a legitimate shuffle. You simply shuffle the selected card from the top to the bottom and back to the top again. It is an easy shuffle to master, and it is deceptive because it looks so much like the shuffle everyone is familiar with. As with any control, do not call attention to what you are doing but simply do it, perhaps describing what is going to happen next or asking someone a question. The more casually you handle the cards, the less suspicious people will be. The selected card is shown with a black border so that it can be followed easily during the explanation that follows.

1. Have a card selected and replaced on top of the deck. Begin an Overhand Shuffle by running one card (the card selected) into your left hand.

2. Follow this single card with a regular Overhand Shuffle until all the cards in your right hand are used up.

3. The situation at this point is that the selected card is now on the bottom, followed by the rest of the deck on top.

4. Start another legitimate Overhand Shuffle.

5. When you are left with a small packet in your right hand, run the cards singly onto the left-hand cards.

6. You will finish with the selected card back on top.

simple overhand control

If you can Overhand Shuffle a deck of cards, you will not have a problem learning this simple method for keeping track of and controlling a chosen card once it has been replaced in the deck. It can be used in conjunction with other shuffles and controls learned previously, but it works best with the Run and Back Control, as the motions of the cards match each other and one shuffling sequence will simply become an extension of the other. The selected card is shown with a black border for ease of explanation.

1. Have a card selected and replaced on top of the deck. Begin an Overhand Shuffle by cutting approximately half the deck from the bottom.

2. Toss this packet onto the selected card as you pull up another group of cards. However, when the first packet is tossed it should be "injogged" approximately 1/2 in (1 cm) back from the top of the deck.

3. Throw the second packet on top, flush with the original packet.

4. As your right hand returns to the deck, the right thumb is able to push all the cards above the selected card forward to grip the original top section of the deck. This is made easy thanks to the "injog."

5. Throw this final packet on top of everything, and the selected card is back on top.

a false cut

This sleight allows you to create the illusion of mixing the cards even though the order of the deck never changes. Used properly, it is a very useful technique to master. There are many different types of false cuts. Some are flashy and difficult to learn; others, like this one, are simple and invisible because it looks as if you cut the deck, when in reality you do nothing!

Success relies on timing the moves so that the cut looks natural. See and feel what it is like to actually cut the cards. Then try and match the look and pace of the real cut while executing the False Cut. Performing a real move before attempting a false move is widely practiced by professional magicians. Once again, the top card is shown with a black border for ease of explanation.

1. Hold the deck facedown up high on the fingertips of the left hand. Your thumb should be on one of the sides, your second, third and fourth fingers on the other side, and your first finger on the end farthest away from you.

2. With your right hand, approach the deck from above. The right first finger lies across the top card, and the thumb and other fingers hold the sides.

3. With the right thumb, split the cards about halfway down. It is the bottom half of the deck that is held by the right thumb; the top half is held entirely (and only) by the left hand.

4. With the right hand, pull the bottom half of the deck away from the top half. The right first finger naturally slides over and off the top card and onto the top card of the bottom packet. This half is cut to the table.

5. The right hand returns to the left and completes the cut by placing the remaining half on top of the cards on the table.

card tricks requiring skill

The following card tricks are a little more complicated than the self-working variety taught earlier. Many of the routines use the techniques previously discussed and will require a certain amount of rehearsal, practice, and dedication to master. As you will notice, many sleights are interchangeable, and you should aim to experiment in order to find techniques that work well for you.

countdown

A card is selected and shuffled into the deck. A spectator is asked for a number, and that number of cards is dealt to the table. The final card dealt is turned over but is not the chosen card. The spectator counts the cards again. This time the last card dealt is found to be the one selected. The method to this trick may seem obvious, but people will be amazed because they do not know about controlling cards.

1. Fan the cards for a selection, stressing the spectator's freedom of choice.

2. Have the card returned and prepare to control it to the top of the deck.

3. You can use any control technique. This is the Simple Overhand Control.

4. Ask for a number between 1 and 52. Deal that number of cards to the table, one on top of the other. You will notice that the first card dealt to the table is the one selected. Assume the number chosen was 14. Deal thirteen cards to the table and turn over the fourteenth card. It will not be the one selected.

5. Act surprised by this failure and reassemble the cards by placing all the dealt cards back on from the top of the deck. As you have just reversed the top fourteen cards, the selected card will now automatically be the fourteenth card down.

6. Give the deck to the spectator and ask him to try. Watch as he deals the chosen number of cards to the table. This time, the final card will be the one selected.

tip If you are able to convince your audience that the selected card has really been shuffled and lost in the deck, the outcome will appear to be a near impossibility. Of course, the best-case scenario occurs if the spectator should happen to choose the number "1." Then you will be able to perform a miracle without having to do anything else – simply turn over the top card. Should this ever happen, stop performing immediately because it is doubtful that anything you do could follow that!

gliding home

This wonderful trick, based on the Glide, is especially good for a large audience. It is a "sucker" trick, which means that the audience thinks the trick has gone wrong when in reality you are in total control. It never fails to amaze people, but it should be performed with a tongue-in-cheek style so as to entertain rather than frustrate or annoy the spectator. Remember, it is all right to fool a spectator, but you should avoid making someone feel or look foolish.

Secret View

1. Spread the cards for a selection, using either a Ribbon Spread or a Two-Handed Spread.

2. Split the deck in half, pushing off the top two cards of the bottom half and holding a Finger Break beneath them. The selected card is replaced on this pile.

3. Once the selected card has been replaced, square the deck, maintaining the Finger Break.

4. Cut all the cards above the break to the table.

5. Place all the cards remaining in your hand on top of the packet on the table. The selected card has now been controlled to the third card from the bottom of the deck.

6. Explain that you are going to eliminate some cards and that you do not want the audience to give you any clues as to whether you are right or wrong. Hold the deck in the left hand, in preparation for the Glide. Tip the deck backward to show the bottom card, and explain that you do not think it is the chosen card.

7. Tip the deck down again and slide off the bottom card of the deck. This resembles the Glide, which you will perform soon.

8. Once again, tip up the deck so that the next card can be seen. Remind the audience not to give you any clues.

9. Deal this card to the table next to the first in a similar fashion.

10. Tip the deck up one last time. This time the selected card will be seen, but continue anyway. Explain that you do not think this is the chosen card.

11. Start to deal this card to the table next to the first two cards. However, you actually perform the Glide so that the penultimate card is secretly removed instead.

Secret View

12. Keep the selected card in the Glide position, and ask for a number between one and ten. Let us assume that "four" is chosen.

13. Deal three cards from the bottom of the deck, using the Glide. The fourth card you pull off is the selection. Hold it toward you and ask which card was chosen. When you hear the response, act as if there has been some mistake.

14. The spectator will rush for the last card you eliminated and will turn it over. She will be amazed to find it is no longer her card. Turn over the card in your hand, and show that you had the correct card all along.

card through handkerchief

A card is chosen and then shuffled back into the deck. The deck is wrapped in a handkerchief and held in the air. Slowly but surely, the selected card starts to melt through the material until it is completely free of the handkerchief. This routine is a classic of magic and visually striking to watch. If performed well, the card really looks as though it is melting through the fabric. The best type of handkerchief to use is a medium-sized gentleman's silk handkerchief of the kind that is usually worn in the breast pocket for show.

1. For this trick, you will need a deck of cards and a handkerchief. Have a card selected and returned to the deck.

2. Using any of the controls taught previously, bring the selected card to the top of the deck. Hold the deck in a left-hand Mechanics' Grip.

3. Cover the deck of cards with a colored silk handkerchief.

4. Reach under the handkerchief with your right hand and remove all but the top card.

5. Place these 51 cards on top of the handkerchief and square them, with the single card beneath. The deck is still held in the Mechanics' Grip.

Secret View

6. Fold the side of the handkerchief nearest you up and over the deck of cards. The bottom card should remain hidden.

Secret View

7. Now fold the material on the right side, underneath the deck. Your left hand will have to alter its grip to accommodate this.

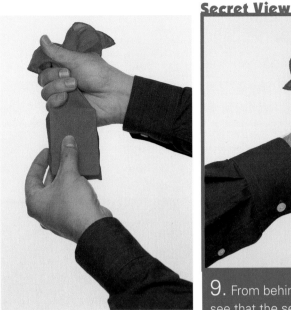

8. Finally, fold the material on the left side, under the deck. Hold the loose corners together in your right hand, out to your right-hand side.

9. From behind, you can see that the selected card is trapped on the outside of the handkerchief, within the folds of the material. The folds stop the card from falling out prematurely.

10. Shake your right hand up and down, and the card will start to emerge. This is the view that your spectators will see from the front.

11. Continue to shake until just before the card falls out completely. With practice, you will know when the card is about to fall free of the handkerchief.

12. Reach up with the left hand, remove the card, and reveal it to be the one selected. The deck can now be unwrapped, and you will be ready to perform another card trick.

cards across

Two packets of ten cards are carefully counted, and two spectators each hold onto one packet tightly. Three cards are caused to fly invisibly from one packet to the other so that when the cards are counted again, one person has seven and the other thirteen. This is a classic of magic for which there are many methods, most requiring some form of sleight of hand. The techniques taught here are relatively simple yet effective. Practice the false counts until you are super-confident with them. They are the key to the success of this trick.

Secret View

1. Hold a deck of cards in your left hand and openly push off ten cards into the right hand. Secretly push off another three cards, obtaining a Finger Break beneath them. Due to the ten-card spread there is a huge amount of cover for this setup.

2. Flip the top ten cards faceup and square them onto the top of the deck. Lift up everything above the Finger Break. You will now be holding ten faceup cards with three facedown cards at the bottom of the packet. Place the rest of the deck off to one side. It is now necessary to count these thirteen cards as ten as follows.

3. Hold the packet in the right-hand Biddle Grip. With your left thumb, pull off the first card and, using the edge of the right-hand packet, flip it facedown onto your left hand, counting out loud, "One." Pull off the second faceup card in the same manner as you place the first card back onto the bottom of the packet. Count "Two." Place this second card to the bottom, as before, and continue counting the cards out loud until you reach the end of the faceup cards. You will have counted ten faceup cards but will have secretly added three facedown cards.

4. Give this packet to the spectator on your left, asking him to hold it tightly between his hands. At this point he will be convinced he is holding just ten cards. Now pick up the deck again, and openly spread off another ten cards, counting each card as you push it off to the right.

5. Lift only seven of the ten cards, and immediately square the sides of these against the cards in your left hand. Don't make a move out of it; just act casually and nonchalantly.

6. Put the deck to one side so that you can recount the seven cards as ten, as follows. Hold the packet in the right-hand Biddle Grip, and use the left thumb to peel off the top card into the left hand, counting out loud, "One." The left hand approaches to move the second card on top of the first, counting "Two." Peel off one more, counting "Three."

7. As the fourth card is taken, place the previous three back onto the bottom of the packet. Do not pause here; just peel off the fourth card, counting "Four." For a second, there will only be one card in your hand when there should be four, but your hands do not stop moving and continue to peel off the fifth card as you count "Five." Continue in this fashion until there are no more cards left. You will have counted seven cards as ten. This false count is not easy, but practice will eventually enable you to perform it without hesitation, which is absolutely essential.

8. Give this packet to the spectator on your right ,and have him hold it securely. Ask each person to confirm how many cards he holds. He should automatically say that he has ten each. Mime sneaking three cards from the spectator on your right and placing them into the hand of the spectator on your left.

9. After this comical byplay, ask the person on your right to count the cards out loud to the table one at a time. There will be only seven cards.

10. The other spectator counts his cards to the table, and incredibly he will now have thirteen!

forcing a card

In many routines, it is necessary to make the spectator take a particular card. Using several techniques explained here, even though you "force" a particular card upon the spectator, the selection procedure seems quite fair and aboveboard. A card force properly executed should arouse no suspicion. Several forces are explained here – in most cases, you can use whichever you feel most comfortable with.

hindu force

This and the Slip Force, which is explained next, are the most practical ways to force a card. The Hindu Force is direct, convincing, and relatively easy to execute. A small amount of practice is all that is required to learn how to do this successfully.

1. The card to be forced should be at the bottom of the deck.

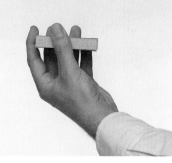

2. Hold the deck high up in the fingertips of your left hand. Your left first finger should be on the outer end of the deck.

3. With the right hand, approach from above and take the bottom three-quarters of the deck away. The thumb is on one side, the second, third and fourth fingers on the other, and the first finger bent lightly on top.

4. Allow the cards in your left hand to fall down to the palm as the right hand returns and the left fingers grab a small group of cards from the top of the deck. Allow these to fall onto the cards below.

5. The bottom card in the right hand always remains the same. Ask a spectator to stop you as you shuffle the deck. When he or she says "Stop," show the bottom card of the packet in your right hand. It will always be the force card.

slip force

This card force is simple yet effective. If performed casually and comfortably, it will be successful every single time. The card to be forced must be on top of the deck at the beginning. It is shown with a black border for ease of explanation.

Secret View

1. Hold the deck in the left-hand Mechanics' Grip. Bend the first finger under the deck, and run your thumb down the corner of the cards. Ask the spectator to say "Stop!" as you riffle through the cards.

2. The right hand approaches the deck from above and grips all the "riffled off" cards. Lift this packet straight up. Pressure is maintained on the top card of the deck (force card) so that it falls flush with and becomes the top card of the bottom half.

3. Tapping the long edge of the right-hand cards on the top of the left-hand cards to square them will add plenty of cover for the move. Extend your left hand, and have the top card (supposedly the card stopped at) looked at and remembered.

cut deeper force

This is an extremely simple way to force a card. However, while this forcing procedure fits some tricks well, it is too laborious to have a card chosen this way every time. In practice, it is highly advisable that the spectator does the cutting and turning of the cards.

1. The card to be forced should be at the top of the deck. In our example, it is the Three of Hearts.

2. Hold the deck facedown in your left hand and cut about a quarter of the cards faceup, replacing them on the deck.

3. Now cut about half the deck faceup and replace that group of cards on the deck.

4. Explain that you will use the first facedown card you come to. Fan through the cards, and cut the deck at the first facedown card. Place all the faceup cards on to the bottom of the deck, turning them facedown as you do so.

5. The top facedown card will be the force card.

cross cut force and prediction

This is a very useful force, easy to accomplish and very deceptive, but only if done correctly. It is taught here as part of a simple trick, as its success relies largely on something known as "time misdirection." This is the concept of using time in between a secret move and the result of that secret move, the idea being that when the spectator tries to reconstruct what happened, she cannot recall the exact sequence of events. Even a few seconds is sufficient. As you will soon see, it would look ridiculous to mark the cut and then immediately reveal the card. The spectator would know instinctively that something illogical had happened.

The back of the force card is here marked with a black border for ease of explanation.

1. When you are ready to start the trick, take a moment to secretly note the top card of the deck. In this example, it is the Six of Clubs. This is the card you will be forcing on the spectator.

2. Begin by giving the cards a shuffle or a False Cut that leaves the top card in position. Either way, the cards should be in front of you, facedown, with the Six of Clubs on top. Explain that you are going to write a prediction. Draw a question mark on one side of a piece of paper and the Six of Clubs on the other side.

3. Place your prediction off to the side of the table but in full view.

4. Ask a spectator to cut the deck at any point into two packets, side by side. It is important that you keep note of where the original top half is placed.

5. Pick up the bottom half of the deck, and place it on the top half of the deck at a right angle. As you do this, explain that you are marking the exact position the spectator cut to, for reference later on.

7. The true orientation and order of the deck will have been forgotten by the time the audience's attention returns. Lift up the top packet, and explain that you are finding the exact point in the deck marked earlier. In reality, you are about to turn over the original top card of the deck.

8. Turn over the supposed cut-to card, and reveal that it matches your earlier prediction.

6. Now "time misdirection" is employed by diverting the spectator's attention away from the deck and onto the prediction. Remind your audience that you made a prediction before the cards were cut and that the cards were cut at a completely random location. Reveal your prediction to be the Six of Clubs.

special gimmicks

There are a variety of specially made playing cards, available from magic shops, which will enable you to perform some amazing tricks. These cards look normal but are faked in some way. Explained here are several special gimmicks you can construct at home. They are not difficult to make, and they give you the ability to show people tricks that they probably have never seen before.

pips away

The Two of Diamonds is picked by a spectator. The card is placed into the center of the deck, and the magician explains that it will magically appear at the top of the deck again. The top card is turned over, but it is the Three of Diamonds. With a flick of the fingers, one of the pips flies off the card, leaving the magician holding the Two of Diamonds!

1. With the help of an adult, carefully cut out one of the diamond pips from a spare card with a craft knife.

2. Attach a tiny piece of reusable adhesive to the underside of the diamond pip.

3. Stick the diamond pip in the center of a duplicate Two of Diamonds so that at a glance it resembles the Three of Diamonds.

4. Set up a deck so that the real Two of Diamonds is on top and the special Two of Diamonds is second from the top.

5. You will need to force the Two of Diamonds using the Cut Deeper Force. Hold the deck facedown on your left hand and ask a spectator to cut off about a quarter of the cards and to turn them faceup on top of the deck.

6. Now ask her to cut about half the cards and to turn them faceup on top of the deck. Explain that you will use the first facedown card you come to.

7. Spread the deck until you come to the first facedown card. That is the force card. Remove all the faceup cards and place them facedown on the bottom of the deck.

8. Lift the top card, and show that it is the Two of Diamonds. Do not look at the face of the card yourself.

9. Push the Two of Diamonds clearly into the center of the deck, and then slowly square the cards.

10. Riffle up the end of the deck, and explain that the chosen card will pass through all the cards and return to the top again.

11. Hold the cards in the left-hand Dealing Grip, and push the top card to the right with your thumb. With your right hand, grip the card at the top right-hand corner so that as the card turns faceup, your fingers are automatically covering the corner pip, which should show "3" but actually shows "2."

12. Turn the card faceup, hiding the far corner pip under your left thumb. Display the special Three of Diamonds, and ask whether it is the chosen card.

13. When the spectator tells you that the chosen card was the Two of Diamonds, say "Watch!" and prepare to flick the center pip with your right finger and thumb.

14. As you flick the pip, it will fly off so fast it seems to disappear, leaving you with the chosen card, the Two of Diamonds.

tip Remember that there is a duplicate Two of Diamonds in the deck, so be sure to remove one of them before handing the deck out for examination.

changing card

A card is selected and shuffled back into the deck. You remove one card from your pocket. It is seen to be incorrect. With a shake of the hand, the card changes into the correct card. As a variation, you could force two cards, in this example, the Six of Clubs followed by the Jack of Spades. Then you can show the first prediction and magically change it to the second.

1. Choose two different cards (in this example, they are the Six of Clubs and the Jack of Spades), plus a spare third card. Fold both of the chosen cards inward with a sharp crease across the center.

2. Glue one half of the folded cards back to back, ensuring perfect alignment.

3. This will create a card that can be shown as either a Jack or a Six.

4. Apply glue to the remaining area of the back.

5. Glue it to the face of the third card. This will strengthen the gimmick.

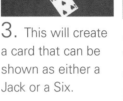

6. Fold the flap into the "up" position, with the Six of Clubs facing outward. Place this card facedown into your breast pocket.

7. Take a deck of cards, and place the Jack of Spades on the bottom in preparation for a card force.

8. Shown here is the Hindu Force, but you can use any force that you feel confident performing.

9. Ask a spectator to say "Stop!" and, then show the bottom card. It will be the Jack of Spades. Shuffle it into the deck and put the cards to one side.

10. Reach into your pocket and remove the fake card, displaying it in your left fingers. Hold it tightly so that the double thickness remains hidden. Ask if you have the correct card. The spectator will tell you it is wrong. Ask which card was chosen.

Secret View

11. Bring your right hand in front of your left, and let the top of the fake card spring forward.

12. As your right hand moves down, allow the flap to open completely so that the card appears to change.

13. Regrip the card so that the entire surface can be displayed. Try to keep the flap aligned.

find the lady

This trick is a famous illegal swindle, often seen played on the streets of cities worldwide, in which people lose their money by betting on the card they believe to be the odd one out. It has many other names, including Three Card Monte and Chase the Ace. Show your friends why they should never play this game.

Three cards are displayed – two eights and a queen. Even though your spectator is sure he knows where the queen is, when he turns over the card, he finds the queen has changed into a joker. With some thought, the Joker can be made to change into many other things.

1. Using scissors, cut a piece off a queen card. The exact size does not matter, but try to cut about a third of the card. It should taper toward one end, as shown here.

2. Trim about ¼ in (5 mm) off the tapered end. This is so that the gimmicked card will work more smoothly, as you will see.

3. Attach a piece of adhesive tape along the back of the long outer edge of the queen, and stick it to one of the eights in a slightly fanned position. The tape acts as a hinge. Experimentation will make this clear.

4. This is how the completed fake card should look.

5. Insert a Joker behind the flap on the fake card and align the edges.

6. Lay another eight on top so that it looks like a fan of three cards. The joker will be completely hidden, and it looks as if you are holding two eights with a queen in the middle.

7. Display this fan of cards, and explain that the spectator simply has to keep his eye on the queen and remember where it is.

8. Turn the fan of cards facedown by turning your wrist, and then ask him where he thinks the queen is. He will tell you it is in the middle. Ask him to remove the middle card.

9. When he turns it over, he will be amazed to find it is a Joker. Close the fan of cards slightly so that you can turn the cards faceup again to flash the two eights.

GLOSSARY

break A small gap between the cards held by a finger or thumb, often used to keep control of a certain card or packet of cards.

cardician An expert card magician or card manipulator.

control The technique of keeping track of one or several cards and secretly shifting the card(s) to another position in the deck.

double lift The lifting of two cards as one.

effect The intended and perceived result of a magic trick.

false cut A cut of the deck that leaves the whole deck or part of the deck in exactly the same order.

false shuffle A shuffle that does not change the order of one or more cards, or that repositions particular cards to other locations in the deck.

flourish A showy, entertaining display of skill or dexterity by a magician.

force The action of influencing a spectator's choice of a card, while making the spectator believe that his or her choice was fair.

gimmick A secret tool that causes a trick to work.

glimpse To take a secret look at a card in a deck.

indifferent card A card whose value is not important.

injog A card that protrudes beyond the end of the deck closest to the magician.

key card A card used to help locate the card selected by a spectator.

packet A small group of cards that is often, but not always, separated from the main section of the deck.

patter The dialogue a magician uses to accompany a trick or routine.

pip One of the small symbols on a playing card.

self-working trick A trick that works by itself, requiring little technical skill or effort on the part of the performer.

sleight The secret manipulation of a card or other object using quick and clever movements of the hands.

spectator A single member of the audience.

sucker trick A trick that appears to have gone wrong but turns out to be a planned part of the presentation. Also, a trick that seems to reveal its secret to the audience but then turns the tables at the last second.

time misdirection The technique of leaving time between a secret move and the moment of magic in order to hide the trick's method.

American Museum of Magic
107 East Michigan Avenue
P.O. Box 5
Marshall, MI 49068
(269) 781-7570
Web site: http://www.americanmuseumofmagic.org
The American Museum of Magic celebrates magicians and their magic. The museum's
    holdings include thousands of magic artifacts and memorabilia. The museum offers
    summer camp programs to introduce young people ages seven to sixteen to the won-
    ders of magic.

Canadian Association of Magicians
Box 41
Elora, ON N0B 1S0
Canada
Web site: http://www.canadianassociationofmagicians.com
This organization promotes and encourages magicians and magic in Canada, through mag-
    ic conventions and other learning and networking opportunities. It is an official member
    of the International Federation of Magic Societies (FISM).

Conjuring Arts Research Center (CARC)
11 West 30th Street, 5th Floor
New York, NY 10001
(212) 594-1033
Web site: http://conjuringarts.org
The Conjuring Arts Research Center is a not-for-profit organization dedicated to the preser-
    vation and interpretation of magic and its allied arts. With its extensive library of books,
    periodicals, and conjuring antiquities, it provides a valuable resource for performers,
    historians, collectors, and the general public.

Genii Magazine
4200 Wisconsin Avenue NW, Suite 106-384
Washington, DC 20016

(301) 652-5800

Web site: http://geniimagazine.com

Founded in 1936, *Genii, The Conjurers' Magazine* is the oldest American magazine for magicians. The periodical appears monthly in both print and digital formats with over one hundred pages of articles, magic tricks, reviews, and more.

MAGIC Magazine
6220 Stevenson Way
Las Vegas, NV 89120
(702) 798-0099
Web site: http://www.magicmagazine.com

MAGIC Magazine is the largest-selling magic periodical in the world. The monthly magazine contains feature stories on the art of magic, in-depth interviews with magicians, and new tricks and effects from some of the most creative minds in magic. It also includes magic news, editorials, and product reviews.

Society of American Magicians (SAM)
Society of Young Magicians (SYM)
P.O. Box 2900
Pahrump, NV 89041
(702) 610-1050
Web sites: http://www.magicsam.com; http://www.magicsym.com

Founded in 1902, the Society of American Magicians is a worldwide organization dedicated to the art of magic. The Society of Young Magicians is its youth branch, serving young people ages seven to seventeen who are interested in learning and performing magic. SYM has "assemblies," or chapters, in locations throughout the country.

Web Sites

Due to the changing nature of Internet links, Rosen Publishing has developed an online list of Web sites related to the subject of this book. This site is updated regularly. Please use this link to access the list:

http://www.rosenlinks.com/MAG/Abra

For Further Reading

Beattie, Rob. *Playing Cards: The Complete Guide to 52 Games, 52 Tricks, 52 Skills*. New York, NY: Metro Books, 2009.

The Diagram Group. *The Little Giant Encyclopedia of Card & Magic Tricks*. New York, NY: Sterling Publishing Company, 2008.

Fullman, Joe. *Card Tricks* (Magic Handbook). Laguna Hills, CA: QEB Publishing, 2008.

Fulves, Karl. *Foolproof Card Tricks for the Amateur Magician*. Mineola, NY: Dover Publications, 2009.

Graff, Lisa. *The Life and Crimes of Bernetta Wallflower: A Novel*. New York, NY: Laura Geringer, 2008.

Hugard, Jean, and Frederick Braue. *The Royal Road to Card Magic*. Mineola, NY: Dover Publications, 1999.

Jay, Joshua. *Joshua Jay's Amazing Book of Cards*. New York, NY: Workman Publishing, 2010.

Jay, Joshua. *Magic: The Complete Course*. New York, NY: Workman Publishing, 2008.

Jennings, Madeleine, and Colin Francome. *Magic Step-by-Step* (Skills in Motion). New York, NY: Rosen Central, 2010.

Kaufman, Richard. *Knack Magic Tricks: A Step-by-Step Guide to Illusions, Sleight of Hand, and Amazing Feats* (Knack: Make It Easy). Guilford, CT: Knack, 2010.

Kieve, Paul. *Hocus Pocus: A Tale of Magnificent Magicians*. New York, NY: Scholastic, 2008.

Longe, Bob. *The Ultimate Book of Card & Magic Tricks*. New York, NY: Sterling Publishing Company, 2006.

Ritchey, David. *26 Card Tricks: For the Intermediate Level Magician Using a Standard Deck*. Terra Alta, WV: Headline Books, 2011.

Turnbull, Stephanie. *Card Tricks*. Mankato, MN: Smart Apple Media, 2012.

Zenon, Paul. *Cool Card Tricks: Techniques for the Advanced Magician*. New York, NY: Rosen Central, 2008.

Zenon, Paul. *Street Magic: Great Tricks and Close-Up Secrets Revealed*. New York, NY: Carlton, 2010.

INDEX

About the Author

Nicholas Einhorn is a "Gold Star'" member of The Inner Magic Circle. In 2011 he "fooled" two of the world's most famous magicians on the UK TV show *Penn & Teller: Fool Us*. He subsequently won a trip to perform alongside Penn and Teller in Las Vegas. Nicholas has won a number of industry awards for his work, including: The Magic Circle Centenary Close-Up Magician 1905–2005; F.I.S.M (World Magic Championships) Award Winner 2003; The Magic Circle Close-Up Magician of the Year 2002; and The Magic Circle Close-Up Magician of the Year 1996. Nicholas performs at events and parties throughout the world as well as uses his magic to build crowds for some of the world's largest companies at business trade shows and exhibitions. Nicholas is regularly invited to lecture at magic societies and conventions the world over. As a magic consultant, Nicholas has designed and created the special effects for several large-scale stage productions as well as being a consultant on several feature films. He also develops and markets new magical effects for the magic fraternity. To date, his illusions have been purchased and performed by magicians all over the world, including some of the biggest names in magic, such as Paul Daniels and David Copperfield.